Enhance Your Chance for Romance

101 Protocols for Online Dating

Brent Louis Miller

Illustrated by Lanessa Miller

Enhance Your Chance for Romance, © copyright, 2017, by Brent Miller.

No part of this book may be reproduced without the express, written consent of the publisher except in the case of brief quotations embodied in critical articles and reviews.

For information, contact Nautilus Publishing,
426 S. Lamar Blvd., Suite 16, Oxford, MS 38655

ISBN: 978-193694663-1

First Edition

Front cover design by Paul Mitchell.

Library of Congress Cataloging-in-Publication Data has been applied for.

Printed in United States of America

10 9 8 7 6 5 4 3 2 1

Table of Contents

Acknowledgments 5
Introduction 7
The New Kismet 9
Think You're Alone? 11
Does Online Dating Really Work? 15
Dating 101 21
In Your Profile 29
A Picture is Worth a Thousand Messages 39
Choosing Who to Date 59
Communicating 71
Meeting in Person 91
Integrity 107
Red Flags 117
Creating Your Profile 139
Photos are Worth Extra Effort! 145
The Survey Says 151
Common Fixes for Common Problems 161
Finally #101 165
Glossary 167
About the Author 171

Acknowledgments

This book evolved over years of my participation in the cyber-world of dating, with all of its ups and downs, and listening to many amusing yet sometimes alarming stories from novice as well as seasoned online daters. I began creating Protocols and Red Flags based on collective experience. This book would not be possible without Julie Schoerke, who has been on the journey with me from the day I decided to become an author; her encouragement has been unwavering. Nor would it be possible without Mary Jo Daly, my editor who patiently worked on wordsmithing.

I appreciate Tim Miller for numerous brainstorming sessions and Todd Metcalf for his input, as well. I am grateful to Neil White and Nautilus Publishing Company for sharing my vision. Thanks, also, to my friends and family who believed in me and supported me on this writing journey.

Special thanks to the late Scott Lockwood for his inspiration and partnership in our 1980s Dial-A-Date venture. And, yes, I must acknowledge all the bad dates I had that made the good dates seem so much better and inspired me to write this book.

Enhance Your Chance for Romance

101 Protocols for Online Dating

Introduction

Enhance Your Chance for Romance: 101 Protocols for Online Dating provides witty, fun Protocols and Red Flags for online dating. The 101 Protocols are easy to read, will make you laugh, and are helpful for both men and women. This book helps even the playing field between novice and seasoned online daters. You will gain insights about the subtleties in profiles and messages that can reveal someone's character and true intent. Learn how to eliminate the fear, gain the ability to forecast a potential date's outcome, and enhance your chance for online romance!

Enhance Your Chance for Romance: 101 Protocols for Online Dating is such an easy and fun read, there's no need to say much more about it. Just start turning the pages and read the entertaining-yet-true tips:

- It's better to lose a lover than love a loser
- Anticipation is an aphrodisiac
- A picture is worth a thousand messages
- Your bait will determine your catch
- Jesus doesn't online date
- Trying to find your cat a date?
- No pics of dead things you've just killed … eek!

The New Kismet

Online dating continues to grow and is more popular now than ever! You probably already interact with Facebook friends, other online buddies, or perhaps LinkedIn business associates that you haven't actually met in person. With the prevalence of texting, apps, and social media, online dating is becoming a normal part of our culture. It's the new kismet! Destiny and fate are not just real-world concepts—they can also happen through a by-chance cyberspace encounter. Meeting someone special you discovered online, and would never have met any other way, is a pretty romantic notion—the proverbial "message in a bottle" gone digital.

Think You're Alone? ...
You're Not

Think You're Alone? ... You're Not

You may be single, but you're not alone—millions of people have learned how to navigate online dating, and you can, too! Here are a few statistics that may surprise you and offer a bit of encouragement:
- Number of single adults in the United States: 54,250,000*
- Total number of adults in the U.S. who have tried online dating: 49,250,000*
- Percent of marriages/current committed relationships that began online: 37%*
- Number of daily sign-ups from just two of the top dating sites: 75,000+

*Source: *Statistic Brain, statisticbrain.com/online-dating-statistics*

If you're thinking about online dating, you may be asking yourself questions like: Who might want to date me? Am I attractive? Why haven't I found the right one yet? Once someone really gets to know the true me, are they going to like me?

Self-doubt is natural. You may need to look inward, perhaps even upward, for answers. The questions may still keep coming:
- Is it normal to online date?
- Are there people out there just like me?
- What will my friends think?
- What if I meet a serial killer?
- Do online dating relationships really last?
- Will I find my happily-ever-after?

The following 101 Protocols can help answer some of your questions. These do's and don'ts are guidelines that will help you navigate the online dating world and have some fun along the way.

Does Online Dating Really Work?

Many people have doubts about the success of online dating. But when you think about it, there are many advantages and only a few disadvantages. It's much like any other type of dating; it just allows you to cast a bigger net. With the help of your computer, cell phone, or tablet, you have access to a whole world of people with whom you may be compatible. Dating sites, social media, algorithms, apps, and more keep changing and growing to accommodate the vast population of single people who want to enhance their chance for romance.

Statistics show that well over a hundred thousand new people sign up for online dating every day. So if you haven't met that special someone yet at the places you frequent—work, church, bars, or restaurants—online dating offers a much larger dating pool.

SPF 30

We all love sunshine. It warms us and lights our world. We bathe in it. It makes flowers grow. Sunrises and sunsets play a key role in many romantic environments.

But even the sun, in all its glory, can burn us. It might seem like a stretch to compare online dating to the sun, but the truth is, they both require some caution and discernment. Whether a day at the beach or a venture into online dating—using the proper amount of screening can help you enjoy the benefits without getting burned. Every rose has its thorns.

When it comes to dating of any sort, there are some stigmas, opinions, fears, misconceptions, and precautions. Your forecast for online dating success will be much brighter when you are armed with the Protocols in this book.

Stigmas

So you think some people frown on online dating. Actually, as we've already seen, the statistics say it's pretty darned popular! And it's your call. Tell your friends you're trying it. Or don't. Many online dating websites allow you to search with many degrees of stealth. So who finds out about it is up to you.

"Résumérs"

Landing a date is much like landing a job. Often, people try to paint themselves in their most positive light. Let's call these people "Résumérs." Expect it. And at least understand that many people feel the need to embellish their own reality. Call it what you will: exaggerations, little white lies, fibs ... It's surprisingly common.

A guy who is 5' 10-1/2" may say he's 6'. A woman who weighs 148 might just claim 135. "Résumérs" may be deceiving themselves more than you. So maybe give a little grace. Even grandma stretches the truth a little bit.

Big Fat Lies

Perhaps lying about weight or height a bit can be forgivable.

But there is a big difference between little white lies and big fat lies. If it is revealed that someone is really 10+ years older than initially claimed, this person obviously deceived you. Use your own judgment and lie meter, but someone who deliberately deceives you about one thing may do the same in several other areas (marital status, criminal record, and other deal breakers). Once someone tells one lie, they may have to tell others to cover it. FYI: Liars are the people who get the most upset when accused of lying.

Don't pave the way for getting into a relationship with a habitual liar, ignoring Red Flags, then wondering how you got involved with someone who hasn't been honest with you since Day 1.

Later, we'll talk about how to identify and avoid Red Flags.

What Online Dating Offers

Online dating offers you more people to choose from and more information about potential matches.

If you just happen to meet someone who sparks your interest, you may start with a couple small-talk questions. It might come off weird or impolite to ask their relationship status or age. It can be embarrassing to ask a person if they are single, and learn that they're not—or worse, discover that they are single, but just aren't interested in you.

Clearly, people on a dating site are interested in dating, and many sites even give you an idea of their intent—whether marriage-minded or something more casual. These are topics that could be quite awkward in many social gatherings when you stumble across an intriguing stranger. Online dating profiles offer a myriad of information about each person. Pictures and a personally written introduction provide a glimpse of their personality, priorities, and interests—far more than you would learn during a mere chance encounter.

Online dating also offers you the chance to communicate with someone as long as you'd like before you commit to meeting in person. Whether your comfort-level includes a long or short getting-to-know-you period, it's all good. YOU are in charge of the searching, screening, communicating, and deciding.

In fact, venturing into online dating doesn't prevent that chance face-to-face meeting with someone special who could still be just around the corner. Once you're open to dating online, you might just find yourself more comfortable and accessible when meeting new people in any situation.

So, to answer the question, "Does online dating really work?"—Yes, it can!

Dating 101

PROTOCOL #1:
Do What You've Always Done, Get What You've Always Got

Admit it, you're single for a reason. Could be that your picker is broken. It's time for a change. Try a new strategy. The one common denominator in all your past failed relationships is you. There is a better way. You have taken your first step toward finding it.

PROTOCOL #2:
I Bet You Never Thought You Would Try Online Dating

But if you're reading this, then you clearly are interested in the possibilities of online romance, if not already active in the online dating world.

It doesn't mean you're desperate, just using one of the tools that God laid before you to find the perfect match. Years ago, there were many ways of meeting potential dates that are no longer available. Let's face it: Invites for lemonade on the front porch pose safety concerns, and no one pitches woo anymore. Perhaps online dating is what replaced them.

And, of course, buy helpful online dating guidebooks that encourage you to consider methods you haven't tried before.

PROTOCOL #3:
Get Outta the Boat!

If you dream of walking on water, the first step is to get out of the boat! There may be a miracle match out there, but you won't find that special someone on or under your couch. Don't be afraid to get out of the boat—you'll float.

PROTOCOL #4:

There are Good Matches and Bad Matches Out There— Bad Ones are Just Much Easier to Find

While online dating, it is easy to get discouraged. Remember, the right one is out there. Online dating is just one of many methods to help you find your perfect match.

PROTOCOL #5:
The View of Memory Lane Looks Better in the Taillights than in the Headlights

Windshields are much larger than rearview mirrors. Headlights are much brighter than taillights. There's a reason for this—to help drive us forward, not backward. One of the keys to online dating success is the idea of a brighter future, so maintaining optimism is paramount. In retrospect, the past sometimes carries a gloss that may not have really existed. Hearts lost in the past encumber future relationships. So leave the past in the past, and focus on creating a whole new set of memories.

PROTOCOL #6:
Consider the Source When Asking Friends for Relationship Advice

Relationally challenged folks always seem to be first in line to deal out relationship advice. Your single friends are likely to tell you to "kick 'em to the curb" upon the first hurdle in the road. They'll rarely understand the chemistry you share with an individual and are not known for their propensity to weather the storm.

In Your Profile

PROTOCOL #7:
Positives Attract, Negatives Distract

Write more about what you want than what you don't want. Beware of having too many negatives in your profile. You may drive away the candidates that actually do meet your stringent, though surely well justified, criteria.

PROTOCOL #8:
Make Every Effort Not to Sound Like a Dumb-Ass (Seek Help if Needed)

Have a friend (preferably smarter than you) proofread your profile; it's better to hear what a dumb-ass you sound like from a close friend than a stranger. Plus, your friends may have some helpful hints and facts you forgot to mention. In most cases, others can speak more clearly about you than even you can.

PROTOCOL #9:
Spell Check!

Your profile is your résumé for your potential date.

It matters. This may sound simple but is often overlooked. Be careful with "you're" and "your;" "their," "they're," and "there;" "whose" and "who's," etc.

PROTOCOL #10:
No Need to State the Obvious

Don't declare your need for honesty and loyalty in your profile. It's a given: Who doesn't want loyalty and honesty? This is commonly found on profiles, and it's pointless to include.

Also, when communicating, don't ask if they're honest. Their answer will always be the same. A person of integrity will declare to you that they're honest—and so will a liar.

PROTOCOL #11:
Driving Past the Gym Every Day on Your Way to Work Doesn't Mean You're at the Gym Every Day

Many people exaggerate how often they exercise. Let your body speak for itself. If running is one of your hobbies and you're looking for a running buddy, it's ok to mention this.

PROTOCOL #12:
No Dollars, No $ense

Keep income details out of your public profile. Unfortunately, some online dating sites require you to enter an income amount. However, most or all of the sites give you the option to keep this information private.

PROTOCOL #13:
Avoid Evangelism

We all have our own beliefs, and they are important to us. But using your profile as a pulpit to try to convert others to your way of thinking will rarely produce a desired outcome. Remember, you have started online dating to improve your life, not everyone else's.

PROTOCOL #14:
Don't Rant About Your Ex-es; that's Why They're Your Ex-es

No one needs (or wants) to hear that. Start with a clean slate; don't let your last relationship ruin your next.

PROTOCOL #15:
Stand Out from the Crowd

Go ahead and check out your competition, because your future date already has. Read some profiles. If you write a generic profile about honesty and a good personality and loving good movies, congratulations—you've put yourself in the same pool with 99% of other online daters! Remember, potential suitors are checking out a plethora of profiles! Strive to stand out from the crowd. You don't want to blend in.

Be specific about your hobbies, your likes, your strengths, even mention your faults: "I is no gud as a spellar." It's a humorous moment that lets potential dates know you are down to earth and real. It can be a great conversation starter.

NOTE: See page 139 for the chapter about how to write your profile.

A Picture is Worth a Thousand Messages

PROTOCOL #16:
No Cheesy Bathroom-Mirror Selfies

You don't socialize in the bathroom, so don't share your private time there with strangers on a dating site. Also, at least give the impression that you have friends who will take your photo. Everybody with a smart phone thinks they're a great photographer. Give them a chance to show off their skills.

PROTOCOL #17:
Your Bait Will Determine Your Catch

Make yourself appealing to the type of person you want to attract through your profile and pictures. We all know it's true that sex sells, but what exactly are you selling?

PROTOCOL #18:
Guys, No Shirtless Pics Next to Your Fancy Car

You're so vain ... Thank you, Carly Simon.

Actually, this is a pretty good rule for women to heed, as well.

PROTOCOL #19:
Women, if Your Pics are of You Lying in Bed, Don't be Surprised When Men Attempt to Join You There

Unless it is your desire to have your inbox filled with messages from men wanting sex, don't use intimately sexy photos as part of your strategy of attraction. And don't pretend to be surprised or offended when men take the bait and approach you in a sexual manner.

PROTOCOL #20:
No Pics of Dead Things You've Just Killed

Advertising murder as one of your best qualities is seldom advisable.

Here's a tip for men that would seem unnecessary, but research reveals quite the opposite. It's laughable that such a large percentage of men's profiles say something like: "My favorite things to do are hunting, fishing, camping, playing football, and watching sports events live and on TV. Looking for a girl who loves the same things."

Really, guys? Sounds like you're looking for a buddy, not a soft, feminine woman to date. Be careful what you wish for …

But women, if you're a sports addict, by all means include it! This will catch more attention than noting that you spend your fall canning pickles!

101 Protocols for Online Dating

PROTOCOL #21:
Don't Haunt Your Own House

Pictures of you with your ex's face blocked out don't belong on your profile. If your most recent pictures still include your ex, you're probably haunting your own house, lamenting the days gone by. Make an effort to get fresh pictures. Astute potential partners will notice that someone's arm is still wrapped around you in the photo.

PROTOCOL #22:
People are Drawn to Enthusiasm

Smile and show some enthusiasm in at least one of your photos. You may hate your smile, but nobody else does. Happiness draws people's attention. Potential matches are attracted to enthusiastic people.

PROTOCOL #23:
Be More than Just a Pretty Face

If all of your photos are taken from the neck up, it may imply that you are hiding something, making potential partners suspicious. Unless your plan is to never meet in person, your date is eventually going to see what you look like. Have a variety of pictures illustrating who you are and be reasonably proud to embrace that you're one of God's creatures. It's better to gain acceptance of your hunchback and lazy eye now than to surprise someone upon first meeting. Avoid the awkwardness of, "Pardon me, are you supposed to be my date this evening?"

PROTOCOL #24:
Clean Your Room Before it's Your Backdrop in Your "This is Me at Home" Pic

The background in your photos says a lot about you and your habits. Someone who doesn't know you yet looks for any clues about your personality. You want your picture to say, "attractive, responsible, organized" instead of, "doesn't know how to operate a vacuum, will refuse to do laundry and dishes."

PROTOCOL #25:
If Your Pics were Taken with Film, You Don't Look Like that Anymore

In this digital era, it is rare for someone to go through the extra effort and expense of using film. It's not impossible that those pics are from last weekend, but let's face it, the guy in the background wearing tube socks, tropical shorts and a mullet is going to tip them off. Use and expect current photos.

PROTOCOL #26:
Refrain from Flaunting Your Breach of Promise

If someone is wearing a wedding band in profile pictures, they are either still married, not over the ex yet, or the pics are old.

There's no need to advertise that you are in breach of your life-long commitment to someone else.

Taking it a step further, when meeting in person, be savvy enough to check the wedding-band finger. If someone has a ring indentation or tan line there, they are likely still married or not enough time has passed.

PROTOCOL #27:
Be Alone in Your Crowd

If you post a group picture, better make it clear which person is you! It's great to have hot friends, but leave them out of your profile pics. Competition is stiff enough!

PROTOCOL #28:
Who the Hell Shot that Picture?

So you've decided to post a candid, rather steamy pic of yourself, half-dressed, bedhead, in the tub, whatever. You are leaving your potential perfect match to wonder—who were you posing for?

PROTOCOL #29:
Money Could be Your Icing But Shouldn't be Your Cake

If your pics are of your material possessions, you're likely a gold digger or about to attract one. Beware of your pics portraying you as materialistic and getting in the way of what really should be important.

PROTOCOL #30:
Don't Post Pictures of You with Members of the Opposite Sex Without an Explanation

It's ok, but not ideal, to include pictures with friends, relatives, or your favorite celebrity in your online photo album. Be sure to clarify who these people are. You don't want inquiring daters to get confused.

PROTOCOL #31:
Elevate, but Don't Exaggerate

In photography: It's really ok to shoot a photo from a higher angle to perhaps hide some portion of your neck that you're not in love with. But ladies, don't tilt the camera so high that all you're showing is an abundance of cleavage and hiding everything else.

Beyond photography: Talk about yourself positively, but not impossibly. Don't tell outlandish stories about yourself. Even if they are true, they won't seem like it, and you don't want to come off all braggadocio right from the start. It's probably best if you don't keep talking about that time you pulled an entire family of four from a burning house, or how you invented the internet, or the fact that yours was the best-looking photo on the post office wall. I think you get the idea.

PROTOCOL #32:
Trying to Find Your Cat a Date?

If you post a picture of your pets, please be holding them or standing next to them. In this case it is all about you. You can mention your relationship with your pets. But don't come off as being the crazy ole cat woman that we all knew as kids.

NOTE: See page 145 for the chapter about profile pics.

Choosing Who to Date

PROTOCOL #33:
It is Better to Lose a Lover than Love a Loser

It's better to be alone than in an unsuitable relationship. You can feel far lonelier in a bad relationship than by yourself if you're with the wrong person. In other words, don't let desperation drive you. It doesn't have a license or any sense of direction.

PROTOCOL #34:
Finding Someone Easy is Easy; Finding Someone Special is Special

Define for yourself: Is it a casual sexual partner, or a lifelong partner you are looking for? Something special is rare, and rare things are much harder to find. Be prepared to put in more time and effort if you want to pull a precious jewel from the rubble.

PROTOCOL #35:
Jesus Doesn't Online Date

Nobody is perfect. Yes, even you are flawed. Determining which flaws you can live with and which flaws you can't requires discernment. If you want others to accept you in all your glorious imperfection, you have to be willing to do the same—you may be surprised how rewarding it turns out to be.

PROTOCOL #36:
Good Things Come to Those Who Wait— but Only the Things Left from Those Who Didn't

Patience is not always a virtue. The fresh bait on the dating site will get plenty of nibbles. Don't wait until the good catch is captured. This isn't a catch-and-release program. The good ones stay caught. In short, the early bird gets the worm.

PROTOCOL #37:
It Ain't All About You

Dating with an agenda of what someone can do for you rarely yields positive results. This type of tunnel vision will likely doom a serious relationship long before it has any chance of sprouting legs. If you need a mechanic or a cook, go hire one. Finding good chemistry should always trump checking off your to-do list.

PROTOCOL #38:
If a Profile Doesn't Have a Photo, They're Likely Hiding Something

At the very least, they are hiding their appearance—and worse, possibly the fact that they aren't single. Sometimes a married person will post a profile to test the waters, but their spouse may not be aware they're contemplating a split and are already out on the prowl. It is not wise to agree to meet with someone without seeing a picture first. It's a digital world—everyone has the ability to share photos.

PROTOCOL #39:
People Get Good at Hiding the Skeletons in Their Closets

If someone seems too good to be true, they probably are. Typically, people are single for a reason. If someone has a problem sharing information about themselves after the initial getting-acquainted period, chances are there is a giant pile of bones that eventually will surface. Don't dive in too quickly, especially if you suspect someone is hiding something or being dishonest. Unfortunately, people sometimes find out they've been dating someone with substance-abuse problems, a spouse, sexual addictions, a criminal past, financial problems, etc. If you have that nagging feeling, it is unlikely that your date is an undercover spy for the CIA. It is more likely that you are being deliberately misled.

PROTOCOL #40:
Those Who Have, Rarely Speak of It. Those Who Don't, Often Do

Beware: Don't believe everything you read. If a person is openly declaring their annual salary in their profile, it is likely not true. Are you interested in a stranger who shares that information with the world?

Bear in mind that internet dating sites don't do background checks or fact-checking. Exaggerating one's income is surprisingly common. So when it comes to other people bragging about their riches on their profile, or in their private messages to you, don't believe everything you read.

Also, don't demand a mate who earns a particular income. Money may be important to you, but you shouldn't mention it in your emails. Your date will find out soon enough that you're shallow.

PROTOCOL #41:
Good Chemistry Can Travel Across the Earth; Bad Chemistry Won't Travel Across the Street

In times past you dated the person down the street because you knew them and your parents knew their parents. If the chemistry wasn't right then you just had to live with it. But those days are gone. Today we cast a much wider net and expect more. We want good chemistry and can and will travel across the earth to get it.

PROTOCOL #42:
Loneliness is Not a Curse, It's a Choice

Don't sit home waiting for a perfect person to come in and change your life. Go out with friends. Accept a date or two. You're not pledging eternal love. Your old ways weren't working, so give people a chance! Doors may open that you never anticipated.

Communicating

PROTOCOL #43:
Don't Use Sexual Innuendos

You might think you're clever or flattering, but it's really best not to lead with sexual innuendos. You don't know the other person yet, so you can't be sure how they will receive it. Here are some examples of cleverly written lines that are still inappropriate:
- You're so hot my zipper is falling for you! ;)
- Do you mind if I end this sentence with a proposition?
- Do you believe in the hereafter? Then you know what I'm here after.
- Nice dress. Can I talk you out of it?

PROTOCOL #44:
Online Dating is a Stepping Stone to Social Interaction, Not for Creating Pen Pals

Search and respond with the intent of meeting someone in the real world. You shouldn't waste others' time, or get their hopes up, if you're always going to hide behind your keyboard. If it's a pen pal you're looking for, there are a lot of lonely prisoners.

PROTOCOL #45:
Don't be Perceived as a Predator

Even if you're an innocent night owl, when sending messages, take note of the time. Messages sent at 3:00 a.m. can come off as the digital equivalent of a booty call, screaming, "I'm trying to score a late-night hook-up." But the same message sent at 7:15 a.m. says that you're motivated and starting your day on a positive note. This is especially true of first-time messages. The time-stamp is part of your first impression; you may not get a second chance.

PROTOCOL #46:
Ignore Dead Ends

Choose only the matches you find most genuinely interesting, and write them a dedicated response. You will eliminate some of your best candidates by not giving them their due attention. Seasoned daters are smart enough to know when you are shining them on.

Don't respond to emails from those who don't interest you. There is no polite or kind way to send a message that says, "I'm looking for a date, but not with you." Responding could easily result in a reply from them, "So, you think you're too good for me?" Or they might say something much worse. This person now has nothing to lose, which could open the door to some ugly reactions, including a few colorful metaphors. It's really best to remain silent and allow yourself to blend into the bevy of other beauties they wrote to that are out of their league.

PROTOCOL #47:
Answers Shouldn't be Shorter than the Question, nor Longer than the Memory of What Was Asked

If someone calls you on the phone or meets you at a public place, make an effort at conversation. For example, if asked where you went to school, an answer like, "U.K.," doesn't tell much. But beginning with, "My earliest memory of pre-school, yadda, yadda, yadda …" is going to get you a glassy-eyed stare. Remember, how you say it is as important as what you say—a lesson many of us forget, but especially true while dating.

PROTOCOL #48:
Quality Over Quantity

Spelled similar, but quite different. You're not running for Homecoming Queen or Class President. You're wanting to make a real connection with a quality person. Don't waste your time or theirs by sending and responding to too many email strings leading to nowhere. As addicting or flattering as it may be to carry on online conversations with many people, use your best discernment and limit yourself to messaging only those you're truly interested in dating. Never underestimate the ability of your potential date to read between the lines.

Also, don't give in to the temptation to answer messages in the shortest way possible just to keep the conversation going. This all too often happens, and any suitor capable of piquing your interest is likely your intellectual equal, certainly intelligent enough to recognize the absence of quality communication and probably will move on to more serious prospects. In any worthwhile relationship, communication requires effort from both people. You are a person of substance. If you're interested in someone, show it.

PROTOCOL #49:
Tell Them They're Attractive, but Don't Dwell on It

Everyone appreciates being told they're attractive. Physical chemistry is a good thing, but it's not the only thing. If you are pleased with a person, switch it up now and then. Compliment their witty sense of humor, their dedication to their career aspirations, and their impressive knowledge of Gilligan's Island reruns. In short, we all like to be appreciated and noticed for something other than our looks.

PROTOCOL #50:
People You Date Should be Fully Aware of Your Marital Status

This goes for whatever your status may be, but is especially for those who are separating from their spouse. Your date doesn't want to hear, "We're going to …" or, "I swear …" Unless you have taken legal action, it doesn't count.

PROTOCOL #51:
Your Caps are Locked!

What you have to say is important, BUT THERE IS NO NEED TO SHOUT IT.

PROTOCOL #52:
Kudos are Free

Kudos often yield high rewards. Be liberal with your praise—but not ridiculous. Everybody loves a compliment. If a person's profile pic with their kids or their pet is so cute it made you laugh out loud, tell them. Even if a profile is written cleverly, it's nice to speak up about it. Or maybe someone listed a quirky habit or hobby in their interests. Don't be afraid to let them know you're paying attention.

PROTOCOL #53:
Understand Anonymity

Despite how wonderful and trustworthy you really are, understand your potential date doesn't know that yet. Safety concerns should prevent folks from being forthcoming with specific personal details, such as workplace, church, address, etc. Be conscious of these types of questions, and don't ask them! You can ask about someone's profession, or which neighborhood or part of town they live in, without asking them to reveal specific locations.

PROTOCOL #54:
Until You Know Someone, Avoid Pet Names

Darlin', Sweetie, Honey, Gorgeous ... These are often used to give the appearance that you know a person better than you actually do. If you commonly use terms like these on people you've just met, then when a relationship ends up being special, the nickname you made up too soon is not so special anymore.

Often, people may find you generically calling them "babe" or "sugar" to be offensive or cheesy.

PROTOCOL #55:
Caution with Your Tone

Do not discard the advantage of being able to re-read your messages before sending. Does this message reflect your true intent? Often, online messages can be misinterpreted and can't be retrieved after the send button has been pressed. Learn to live with the fact that if it can be misinterpreted, it will be.

PROTOCOL #56:
People Like to Talk About Themselves —Let Them

Evaluate your communication skills. No one likes a one-sided conversation, and if your date doesn't know this, it may be a reason for pause. God gave you two ears and one mouth for a reason.

PROTOCOL #57:
Be Better than the Same Ole Generic Blah, Blah, Blah ...

Show an interest in the important details someone chooses to share in their profile. If you know their name, use it. You can say something like, "I see you love horseback riding, Mary. I went riding last Sunday." Your personal approach will be noticed and is likely to receive a much more dedicated response. You can be sure this hottie is receiving lots of messages, but taking a genuine interest will put you in another league from the many who just send generic babble like, "Hey, good lookin'. How ya doin'? Blah, blah, blah ..."

PROTOCOL #58:
Get Real!

If you're 58 and out of shape, stop messaging the 21-year-old super-hotties. You had your chance years ago. Now it's someone else's turn. Ambition is good, but let's be realistic.

PROTOCOL #59:
Squash Any Illusion of Enlightenment

If you have been on a few dates and they all seem to be turning out badly, then you may just start asking yourself, "Why do people maintain such bad behavior and wonder why they haven't found anyone yet?" Any attempt to enlighten these folks will likely end badly. (Don't ask how I know.) So just be secure in the fact that you know better and c'est la vie.

PROTOCOL #60:
Anticipation is an Aphrodisiac

Don't reveal too much too soon. Leaving more to the imagination is attractive. It is considered good dating practice not to expose too much of yourself, or all of your amazing qualities, too soon. But remember, smart dates may be playing by the same rule.

PROTOCOL #61:
Take It Offline When You're Not Strangers Anymore

So you're past the original getting-to-know-you period. You've already met someone in person, and you're exchanging emails, texts, and phone calls. You've now graduated to real-world relationship status and grown out of the need for messaging via the online dating site. The dating websites are designed to let folks chat while remaining anonymous.

Continuing to send messages through the online dating portal can stir the pot of questions: Are you stalking your new interest by checking how active they are online? Are you still conversing with many others online? Did you only message the person because you ran across their profile while you were surfing for other prospects?

Also, many of the dating sites allow people you are actively messaging to see when you are online. This can create unnecessary, unwanted drama.

Meeting in Person

PROTOCOL #62:
Can't Replace Face to Face

You might feel like you're sitting on a powder keg of chemistry via messaging, email, text, and talk. But nothing can replace the magic of great chemistry during your first face-to-face meeting with that potentially special someone. The word that comes to mind is "smitten." You can't always describe it, but you know it when it happens. Research for this book revealed hordes of folks that felt a magnetic attraction via messaging, but mysteriously, there was no spark during their first face-to-face encounter. But take note, several married couples that met online revealed that the reverse can often happen, as well. You never know if fireworks will fly until you actually get up close and personal. So, keeping safety concerns in mind, don't postpone that first face-to-face meeting for an extended time.

101 Protocols for Online Dating

PROTOCOL #63:
Avoid That Deer-in-the-Headlights Moment

If you are ready to meet someone you're chatting with, and you truly believe this relationship has legs, then choose the location for your first date wisely. Later, you may prefer not to announce to the world that you met through an online dating site or that your first date was in a smoky bar. For years to come, people will ask, "Where did you two meet?" Avoid the awkwardness of looking like a deer in the headlights while searching for something to say. You'll need a truthful answer without revealing too much. While you were both waiting to be seated at a nice restaurant may be just the ticket—still the truth without TMI.

PROTOCOL #64:
The Where, the Wear, the Wow

At your first meeting, you can control many factors that make a long-term first impression. Where you meet and what you wear are all part of that WOW factor you are striving for.

Neither crowded bars nor quiet movie theaters are great environments to carry on a conversation and really get to know each other.

What you wear makes an impression. There is no one sartorial rule that universally applies, but laundered, unwrinkled clothes are kind of a given. Avoid extremes: too tight, too short, too sloppy, too much cologne, etc.

Ladies: It's ok to accentuate your figure. But if you are dressed in such a manner that you are basically "leading" with your boobs, then don't be offended when your date notices, and keeps noticing. Guys: It's ok to catch a glimpse, but don't stare!

A wardrobe choice that works for every occasion: Wear your smile! It's uniquely yours and rarely forgotten.

PROTOCOL #65:
You're Seeking an Investor in Your Future, Not Hiring Someone for the Job

It's easy to fall into the snare of interview-style dating, seeking the best person for the job. You would not have the same conversation with a job candidate that you would with a potential investor. It may seem a bit analytical, but a relationship works much like a business, where a group of people (in this case two) works together with a common goal. Often, businesses are a 50/50 partnership. But a relationship is 100/100. Both need to be all in, investing in each other. No subordinates—a partnership of equals.

PROTOCOL #66:
Be a Glass-Half-Full Person

This is an especially big problem for seasoned online daters. After kissing a few frogs and not getting your prince, without realizing it, one can become a bit bitter. We've all had our share of bad dates. Don't become a victim of your own past mistakes. Rise above it. Everybody prefers to spend time with a person who looks on the bright side. You shouldn't have too-firmly-planted rose-colored glasses on your nose, but a tint of pink can be pretty attractive on you! Assume the best until the worst is imminent.

PROTOCOL #67:
Engage with Your Date, Not Your Phone

We all know we shouldn't, but we've all done it. Being distracted by our phones is just plain rude. Ignore texts, emails, and calls while on a date. Exceptions exist, but they are rare. Put your phone away, out of sight. Keeping it on the table in front of you can be very distracting and may cause unwanted drama—especially if your date sees several messages come in from possible other suitors. If you must check for important messages, do it discretely during a break in the conversation. Or perhaps let your date know, in advance, that you may be expecting an important call from your boss or a family member. If someone takes the time to meet you, they deserve your focus.

PROTOCOL #68:
Cooking Up Chemistry

If you're attracted like two refrigerator magnets when you first meet, exercise a little self-control! Upon further discovery, your conversations could reveal some real deal-breakers. So don't let your libido write checks that your morals will regret cashing. That first night of passion may seem uniquely spontaneous, but later you both will wonder if your date routinely participates in such behavior.

PROTOCOL #69:
Dance with the One Who Brung Ya

Sometimes it's tempting to try to meet more than one date at a single event. If you commit to an outing with someone, don't flirt with the waitstaff or go MIA in hopes of a better "catch." It's just plain tacky.

PROTOCOL #70:
If You Don't Click With Your Date, Offer to Pay Your Own Way

If you've just met someone and you're just not that into them, then going dutch won't come off like you just wanted a free meal.

PROTOCOL #71:
They'll Notice You Noticed

Lots of the Protocols are about what *not* to do. This is a tip about what *to do*. If you're lucky enough to get the second date, mention some positive detail about your dating partner at your previous meeting/date. This may seem like a small thing, but it can have a big impact.

Most ladies put quite a lot of effort into accessorizing and other subtle details when getting ready for a date. She may have changed her jewelry or hair three times to impress you. She will appreciate when you notice her choices. Mention that the blue earrings she wore looked great with her blue top. The flattering way she wore her hair. Her shoes matched her belt. You loved her scarf, broach, or bracelet.

This isn't just for the men. Ladies: Maybe tell a man you really appreciated his manners when he opened doors for you, or waited to make sure your car started before he left the parking lot. Letting a guy know you appreciate his gentlemanly conduct will not only flatter him but could actually reinforce this positive behavior.

Noticing small details about your last encounter will get you noticed. Kind remarks get remembered and have an impact, when sincere. This allows you to stand out. You'll be surprised what an impression it will make.

PROTOCOL #72:
Sequestered Juries Don't Deliberate

After a first meeting, if your date can't decide if they want to get together again, move on. If you don't get a smiling, excited yes, it's a no. Waiting for deliberation has the nectar of desperation.

PROTOCOL #73:

Get to Know Your Date Before Your Date Gets to Know Your Children

If you're going to introduce someone into your children's lives, do so with the intention of keeping them there. You would only introduce a partner to your own parents when the relationship becomes serious. Think the same way when it comes to your own children.

Integrity

PROTOCOL #74:
The Anonymity of a Keyboard May Hide the Lack of a Spine

People often will type things to a person they would never say to their face. Avoid those who resort to being rude or lewd with only their keyboard. Most dating sites offer the ability to block members from communicating with you. Exercise your right to block the blockheads!

PROTOCOL #75:
Any First-Grader Can Cut and Paste

Beware of serial daters. If the first message you receive from a person doesn't include your screen name, or reference to your profile in any way, that exact same message was possibly sent to several different people. Serial daters often play the numbers game. More inquiries = more dates. Same message, many different people. You're worth a personal message!

Integrity

PROTOCOL #76:
Don't Disrespect Others, and Don't Tolerate Those Who Do

One can be judged by the way they treat others that can do nothing for them. Pay attention to how your date treats the wait staff, the person behind the counter, and other folks they're not trying to impress.

PROTOCOL #77:
Sleeping on the Couch Doesn't Make You Single

If you're still living with your spouse, no matter where you're sleeping, you're not single! You may really be on your way to a permanent split, but you're not there yet. Trying to snare a new lover before you're living under a separate roof from your previous one will raise a lot of questions about the quality of your character in the eyes of any worthwhile prospects. Trying to pick up a new squeeze when your emotional baggage actually includes a set of packed suitcases will only further complicate the crucial first moments of a new relationship.

Integrity

PROTOCOL #78:
If You Show Me Yours, You'll Never See Mine

Just a heads-up that some men (or "creepers" as they are more commonly known) send pictures of their Johnson (AKA penis) to women they have never met. Not your dream date. Trust me, you're not the first one.

This tactic may seem ridiculous, but men still do it. This never works. Their true intent is: "I'll show ya mine if you show me yours." Most women, of course, want the WHOLE package: mind, body, and soul.

PROTOCOL #79:
If an Escort is What You're Seeking, There are Other Sites for That

Legitimate online dating sites are geared toward building serious, lasting relationships. Some people use the same sites to search for sex hook-ups. If that's all you want, there are plenty of other websites created for that specific purpose.

PROTOCOL #80:
If You're Unemployed, Look for a Job, Not a Date

If you can't take care of yourself, you can't take care of a partner. Not everyone has the career of their dreams, but having any job is always preferable to no job.

PROTOCOL #81:
Geographic Location Does Not Grant a Pardon for Infidelity

Divorce is determined by a judge, not by your geographic location.

Just because you're in a different zip code doesn't mean it's not cheating. Don't allow yourself to be the other woman (or man). Like it or not, a lot of people on dating sites are married! If a relationship is what you desire, don't let yourself become action-on-the-side.

PROTOCOL #82:
Be Kind—You're Not the Only One Having a Hard Time with This

Dating of any kind is usually a rough process for everyone. Remember, we're all human. Follow the golden rule of treating others as you would like to be treated. Be respectful and considerate in your conversation and emails, whether it's the first meeting or the 29th date. Things that you find easy may be difficult for other people, and the reverse is likely true as well.

Red Flags

If any three of the following statements are true about a person, then you probably shouldn't date them. It's a "three strikes you're out" kind of thing.

THESE ARE RED FLAGS, IF THE PERSON YOU ARE CONSIDERING DATING ...

PROTOCOL #83:
Has Changed Phone Numbers More Than Twice in the Past Year

What does this say about someone? They didn't pay their bill, again? They are hiding from the past—from someone or something that they don't want to find them?

PROTOCOL #84:
Asks for Your Address Before You Have Actually Met

If someone asks for your address before you've met each other, they may be concerned that you won't want to give them your address once you meet. Be cautious: Don't have someone pick you up at your place on the first few dates. Remember, a person's criminal record is not listed in their dating profile! Your address is a need-to-know piece of information. And no one needs to know, yet! If someone wants to know where you live to determine a convenient place to meet, just give some nearby cross-streets or a familiar landmark.

PROTOCOL #85:
Resorts to Name-Calling When Describing Their Ex

The obvious fact is, that ex previously held a very special place in their life. The uglier the talk about the ex, the redder the flag. Remember, someday YOU may be that ex to whom they are referring.

PROTOCOL #86:
Doesn't Know Their Mom's Birthday

The most important person in someone's life, for many, many years, is mom. A sure sign of self-absorption is the inability to keep track of this one very special occasion. It is likely a mere drop in the bucketful of other really important things that will remain forgotten.

PROTOCOL #87:
All Their Problems are Someone Else's Fault (Blamers)

There are two sides to every story. Bad past relationships are never all one person's fault. We are each responsible for our own actions and the place we find ourselves along life's journey. Those who consistently believe that everything is somebody else's fault have difficulty finding happiness. They look to someone else to be the source of their happiness. When they are unhappy, they look for someone to blame. Bad things happen to all of us. How one reacts makes all the difference. Beware of this victim mentality in others. Next thing you know, you will be the scapegoat, and this person will, again, play the victim. Avoid blamers—and don't be one, either.

Red Flags

PROTOCOL #88:
Refuses to Speak to One or More Immediate Family Members

Someone unwilling to set aside differences with their own blood demonstrates the inability to overcome pettiness. And it's likely that YOUR family will fare far worse.

PROTOCOL #89:
Is Wearing a Hat and/or Sunglasses in All Profile Pics

First of all, do you want to date someone whose face you haven't really seen? Second, what are they hiding (a receding hairline)? Third, do you really want to date someone who hasn't taken this dating process seriously enough to post a decent picture? Maybe some guy thinks he's Joe Cool, and in all his pics he's wearing a hat and dark shades. What's next, a pirate with an eye patch? Arrggh.

Red Flags

PROTOCOL #90:
Doesn't Own a Suit/Dress
(or at Least a Sport Coat and Tie)

Special occasions often require us to dress to impress. Dating someone who is unwilling to do so could exclude you from the guest list of many future fun events. If someone doesn't own at least one pair of dress shoes and tennis shoes, this is a lifestyle choice, more than a wardrobe choice.

The informalness of tennis shoes might be a little awkward at Aunt Bertha's wedding, the company Christmas party, or the occasional fine-dining that you may want to experience.

On the other extreme, how fun would it be to date someone who is so highbrow that they never strap on a pair of tennis shoes?

PROTOCOL #91:
Photos Show a Lot of Skin and No Face

The profile is filled with sexual innuendos, just pics of body parts or tattoos, and/or says little to no "normal" stuff about dating. If you are just looking for a hook-up, you might want to respond to this type of profile. But if you are looking for a real relationship, better pass.

PROTOCOL #92:
Quits Their Job Before Finding Another One

We've all had a jerk for a boss at some point. Rarely does a job exist where you are not, at some point, upset with the boss. If someone gets mad, quits, and storms out the door, this speaks volumes about their character. They will likely do the same thing when any relationship hits a bump in the road.

PROTOCOL #93:
Has Kids They Haven't Seen in More Than a Year

Family is important. That's not just an old-school idea. If your potential date has shunned his children, you might not fare so well either, eventually.

PROTOCOL #94:
Has Been in Jail More Than Once

Everybody makes mistakes. Accidents can happen. Misaccusations can occur. But lightning doesn't strike twice.

Red Flags

PROTOCOL #95:
Is More Than 20 Minutes Late Without Calling

Remote locations aside, these days most people can send a quick text or make a quick call on their cell phone. Dead batteries and glitches can happen. But tardiness with no contact may be due to lack of respect, not lack of signal.

PROTOCOL #96:
Has Never Dressed Up for Halloween (or Some Other Costume Event)

Everyone enjoys a special occasion once in a while. Sometimes these occasions require some type of dress-up or costume. The inability to go with the flow and make fun of oneself could demonstrate the lack of flexibility often needed as part of a good relationship.

PROTOCOL #97:
Uses the "N" And The "F" Word

It doesn't take Einstein to know that it's unacceptable to use the "N" word, refer to gay people as "fags," etc. Such blatant closed-mindedness demonstrates hate and insensitivity to those who are different. Furthermore, it shows an ignorance of political correctness. Such language is disrespectful toward others. Remember, you, too, could soon be the target of such disrespect.

PROTOCOL #98:
Doesn't Have a Credit Card or a Checking Account

It's not necessary to demonstrate why a person needs these. The question is, what is the true reason behind someone NOT having them? You find a few nonconformists who insist they are rebelling against "the system." More likely, the system ejected them for very good reasons.

PROTOCOL #99:
Uses More Than One Form of Tobacco

Some folks don't mind this, but have you ever planted a kiss on someone you didn't know had a mouthful of chewing tobacco? Clearly, this person is not health-conscious and isn't doing much to take care of the pearly whites. E-snuff said.

PROTOCOL #100:
Doesn't Plan to Fail, Just Fails to Plan

Brighter futures don't happen by accident. They happen by design. You may potentially be a part of this person's future. So it's a great idea to pick someone who has a great future in store.

> "I love it when a plan comes together."
> ~ Col. Hannibal Smith, *The A-Team*

Creating Your Profile

Still scratching my head about why folks put so little effort into writing their profiles and hope to find the person of their dreams. You spend at least 12 to 18 years getting an education in expectation of obtaining happiness through a good career. Doesn't it make sense to spend at least 12 to 18 minutes concentrating on your profile? Finding an ideal mate will more likely yield a better chance of happiness than all the education in the world.

This Is Not An Autobiography—Conversely, This Is Not A One-Liner

In your profile, tell some details about yourself so someone can begin to get to know you. But you're not writing a book! You can't really expect someone to read and remember ten pages of detailed information. Conversely, a short, generic profile won't be taken seriously. If you are truly interested in meeting someone special, take the time to write a compelling introduction to yourself. Keep in mind the proper amount of brevity.

Who are you?

When describing yourself to potential suitors, you're not trying to appeal to the masses. Refer to Protocol #15: Stand Out From The Crowd. Ultimately, you're trying to appeal to just one very special person. Your mission is not to cast a big net, and catch a big haul of fish. Your objective is to cast a specific net, and catch a very specific fish.

Your first instinct may be to list some general, surface qualities about yourself: "I'm honest, loyal, and down-to-earth." This is your opportunity to introduce yourself and provide an impression of who you really are. You need to share a little of your personality, priorities, interests, and outlook on life if you want your profile to sound unique.

Honey vs. Vinegar

Highlight your best qualities. Use positive words like fun-loving, responsible, friendly, spirited, respectful, confident, ambitious, happy, enthusiastic … Of course, only use the words that truly apply to you.

Consider being a little playful or lighthearted with your words. If you are the kind of person who doesn't take yourself too seriously, maybe refer to yourself as a girl, or boy, or a kid at heart.

If your profile is full of "don't" and "never" and other negative words, consider rephrasing. Statements like, "I don't want to date someone who …" or "I never date smokers …" come off very negative. This could be a turn-off to the positive people you want to attract.

Try to focus on the positive qualities you seek. "I am health-conscious and a non-smoker and prefer to date someone like-minded." You catch more flies with honey than vinegar.

If you find someone appealing, so will many others. A negative first impression could give them a reason to move on—before you've even had a chance to say hello! Refer to Protocol #7: Positives Attract, Negatives Distract.

While it's great to paint yourself in a positive light, you don't want to create Red Flags by being deliberately deceptive. A relationship which is somewhat based on half-truths will have a shaky foundation and a limited life-span.

Peanut Butter & Jelly

If you are seeking a required list of traits—age, height/weight, profession, etc., you are sure to miss out on some wonderful people who you might have thought aren't your "type."

It's not a good idea to create a mold or template and expect to find the person who fits in it. Remember, your dating criteria have not worked in the past, so take this opportunity to change it up a bit. Be open to the idea of dating someone who is different than you. Two people can complement each other when they are good at different things. What would peanut butter be without the jelly? Sugar without the spice? Meat without potatoes? Or the moon without the sun? I think you get the idea. Two very different things often make a great pair.

Still Having Difficulty Writing Your Profile?

Here is an idea: If you have a hard time writing about yourself, have someone else write it.

It starts: If you were to get to know my friend "Kelly," you would find out how _____ she is. And knowing her like I do, you would also discover _____ and etc.

NOTE: See page 29 for profile Protocols.

Photos are Worth Extra Effort!

It's almost impossible to stress strongly enough how important good photos are! Your photo is your first and best shot of capturing someone's attention when online dating. It is your profile pic that entices someone to click and read more about you. Your dream date will never get to know how wonderful you really are unless your smiling face motivates them to click.

You'll find I mention the need for great photos repeatedly in this book. I am a professional photographer. I am not trying to drum up business for myself and my cohorts. I just know, firsthand, how amazing someone—YOU—can look with proper framing, lighting, angles, a shallow depth of field, etc.

I promise you, professional photographers utilize plenty of tricks of the trade to make everybody look their very best.

People have a hard time being objective about their own photos. Ask some close friends. They care about you and can help you choose the photos that are the most flattering and interesting. While you may love certain pics of yourself, others may tell you they're too artsy-fartsy, or ask "Why aren't you smiling?," or say it looks like you take hundreds of selfies. They will likely expose you to ideas that you weren't even considering.

If you resort to a bathroom selfie, folks may pass on the opportunity to read about the great chemistry the two of you may have. (Refer to Protocol #16: No Cheesy Bathroom-Mirror Selfies.) If you must resort to selfies, at least close the toilet seat and the shower curtain. Or CROP! Oh, and here's a hint if you're having a hard time. If you are taking a picture of your reflection in a mirror, look in the mirror, not the camera. It might not seem like an IQ test, but my market research shows that many people (admittedly, mostly us men) can't figure out this concept.

Variety

At least one of your pictures should be a headshot—a nice photo of your smiling face. Some should be body shots—showing you standing, head to toe, if possible. Additional pictures should be action shots—showing you doing something you enjoy, something you love: playing baseball, dancing, interacting with your pets, enjoying recent travel destinations, etc.

Rotation

Ideally, you want to have 10-12 photos of yourself. But you won't be posting all of them at one time. Post only three photos at a time. By rotating your photos periodically, every ten days or so, you keep your profile fresh and interesting. Like bread, photos can get stale if you leave them on the shelf too long. Rotate the three photos that are displayed on your profile. You will be surprised at how much more attention that gets. Maybe last week's photo just didn't quite do it for someone who meets all your search criteria. But your new photo displaying your latest travel adventure may be just the ticket that captures the attention of your perfect dream date.

Why Photos Are So Important: The 80/20 Rule

How the 80/20 rule applies to online dating: The people who are looking for an online date only click on a profile and read more if they are attracted to the main photo. Approximately 20 percent of the photos get about 80 percent of the clicks! You want to be in that 20 percent of photos that get clicked. The other 80 percent of members on the dating site get passed by, likely because of poor quality photos. Make sure your interesting pictures draw in your potential suitors so they read your clever, warm profile.

Take Your Best Shot

Make an extra effort to acquire your best photo. You would be surprised how amazing you will look and how much fun you will have in a professional photo shoot! Make a day of it. Get a mani/pedi and get your hair done. Bring a friend. Smile. Sparkle. Have fun!! Professional photographers work hard at making their photos better than anything that can be shot with a smart phone. They get paid to make you look fabulous! And they're good at it, or they wouldn't be in business very long. A professional photo shoot is surprisingly affordable. Look for ads, discounts, and coupons. A good photo of yourself can be useful for business, to share with family, social media, and lots more.

Do-It-Yourselfers

Of course, if this is all intimidating to you and beyond your budget, then recruit a friend with the best camera you can find to shoot you in your best light. Here are some tips from a professional photographer (me):

• Posture is extremely important! Try this: Stand up straight. Raise your shoulders up by your ears. Then push your shoulders back. Then drop them down. A tip to remember this: Shoulders Up. Back. Down.

• Bright eyes make you more photogenic. Consider using a little Visine or similar eye-whitening product right before the shoot.

• There's a trick to avoid red-eye. In dark areas when using a flash, look at a light source just before the photo is taken. This shrinks the pupil. Large pupils are the most common cause of red-eye.

• Ladies: Unless you are super-model thin, it's best not to

be photographed in sleeveless clothing that exposes your upper arms. It's true what they say, the camera adds 10 pounds—often in this area, and most don't want to look like they weigh more than they really do.

- Avoid at all cost: muffin top! Sometimes ladies tend to wear snug-fitting pants to show off their curves. This can cause a very unflattering bulge over the waistline. A quick, cheap solution: Saran Wrap. Certainly not a permanent remedy.
- Be careful when using flash photography. The flash reflection in nearby mirrors, windows, glass, chrome, etc. creates a glare that can be a distraction and can even alter exposure, causing lighting problems.
- Include some attractive and uncluttered foreground and background.
- Shoot outside from a slightly elevated angle, and with the subject slightly off-center.
- SMILE!

NOTE: See page 39 for photo Protocols.

The Survey Says ...

The Survey Says ...

Several online dating sites served as a testing ground for some of the theories and ideas presented in this book. Some of the test profiles yielded noteworthy results.

If You're Getting Too Many "Hey Baby" Messages, Consider Using A Hidden Test

Want to make sure the people who contact you have actually read your profile? Consider putting a "hidden message" inside your profile. The test we used in our market research went something like this: "If you have taken the time to read my profile and decide to contact me, please call me by my name: (Insert your name here, or a nickname, or a name you like to be called.)"

Or perhaps make up your own test. "My favorite color is purple. Please use the word 'purple' in your first message to me, so I know you were courteous enough to read my profile. And please, tell me your favorite color, too." Using a test like this will help you weed out the people who haven't taken the time to read the information you wanted them to know about you. And it can give you a fun conversation-starter, as well. Try it!

The truth is, most serial daters don't read profiles; they only look at pictures. Do you really want to date people who are so shallow that they are only interested in your looks? We've all heard our fair share of pick-up lines, and sending someone a message without reading their profile is the online equivalent of walking up to a stranger in a bar with a bad line.

FYI: Our market research revealed the top two first messages men sent to women, while ignoring the hidden test inside the profile: "Hey, beautiful." And "Hi, gorgeous." These sentiments may seem flattering, and they aren't necessarily wrong or offensive. But if that is the entire message, and the sender ignored your hidden test, that message was likely sent to multiple people. Refer to Protocol #75: Any First-Grader Can Cut And Paste.

Experiment #1: "Doreen" Vs. "The Anti-Doreen, Samantha"

The following two test profiles yielded especially interesting results.

Test Profile #1: "Doreen"

A test profile of a stunning young lady, "Doreen," featured professional photos that showed her at her very best.

But that was the only thing about Doreen that was at her best. Doreen described herself as a frequent drinker, frequent smoker, social drug user with no job and no car. She listed a high-school education, "separated" as her marital status, and her longest relationship was just over one year. Doreen came off as a total egocentric diva, a racist, a gold-digger, and frankly, a real b*tch. Doreen also made it very clear that she wasn't giving up any sex until she had a very expensive wedding ring on her finger and became a pampered wife, living in an upscale home with servants and a purse full of credit cards.

Here Is Doreen's Test Profile:

Are all men total losers? I am gorgeous, smart, and deserve to be treated like a queen.
- If you ain't white, you ain't right.
- If you ain't educated, do not bother me.
- If you a mamma's boy, stay home with yo mamma.
- If you ain't in fine physical form, move on.

Take me shopping, hold my hand, hold my purse, and I'll hold your wallet.

A woman like me should be put on a pedestal. I want a real man who takes care of his woman. I'm looking for long-term, a man who is husband material. You should be self-sufficient, financially and otherwise. I'm not your cook, I'm not your maid, I'm not your nurse or your nanny. I will not be treated like the hired help. I am the classic material girl. Our future together will include an upscale house and life's finer pleasures. I will not settle for less! If you have taken the time to read my profile and hope to possibly date me then call me by my name and it is Doreen. If not, I won't respond. Call me a snob or a diva, but I'm worth any three of your past dates.

Don't think I will share your bed with you if you don't meet my standards. If ya like it, put a ring on it – no sex till we're married and even then it will be only on special occasions.

My Interests: Shopping, Travel, Theatre, Ballet, Opera, Symphony, Barry Manilow, Designer fashion, Expensive jewelry

Our First Date: Upscale dining, theatre, don't think you are getting away with just buying me coffee.

Colorblind

Interestingly, Doreen's overt racism did not stop several people of color from contacting her. In fact, the first response to Doreen's profile came from a suitor who called himself "Proud Mexican."

Ya Never Even Call Me By My Name

In the vast majority of messages, it was quite obvious that the sender did NOT read Doreen's racist profile. Not only did their clueless enthusiasm reveal that they did not read the pretty girl's ugly comments, but they failed a test inside her profile. Buried within the profile was this sentence: "If you have taken the time to read my profile and hope to possibly date me, then call me by my name: It is Doreen. If not, I won't respond."

The Clueless Masses

Less than nine percent of respondents used Doreen's name in their message to her. Most of those sending messages were blinded by her beauty, never bothering to read her ugly comments nor the hidden clue to mention her name.

Only one person actually called Doreen out for her b*tchy attitude. He clearly read the profile; he called her by her name.

A few guys kinda/sorta alluded to Doreen's less-than-pleasant attitude. However, they were very polite about it, dancing around the issue, seemingly still holding out hope for a date.

Here Are Some Messages "Doreen" Received:

- "You had me really interested until the last 4 words. I treat whoever I'm with like a queen but I also like being treated like a king. I probably live too far away anyway."
- "Hi. My name is ross.how r u today"
- "Not only r u freak'n beautiful and sexy but, ur not tainted"
- "You're absolutely stunning. I know there's a some distance but between us but I just feel like we owe it to any future children we might have to get to know each other sooner rather than later ;)"
- "Hello Ms. 72 Inches of Sugar & Spice (in your sexy stilettos),

Your profile has a little more spice than sugar but, I happen to like a strong, dominant women. I am an alpha male but, interested in a female-led relationship which she provides discipline, determines when I release and makes the rules. Have you ever been in a relationship like this? Hope to hear back."
- "I am direct. I am sure of what i like. I like sports. I like

conversation. I like to listen. I like to have fun. I like romance. I like going out or staying in. I played some college ball. I worked in the IT filed, and I would really like to take you out on a date sometime? Well that is all I can come up with now got to run, Hope to hear back soon"

Test Profile #2: The Anti-Doreen, "Samantha"

Here is the other side of the spectrum, our "anti-Doreen," named "Samantha." This experiment is about the importance of good pictures. So, Samantha's pictures were terrible. Her main image showed her in mid-blink on a super sunny day—wincing into the sun. A second picture captured an unflattering angle, showing a slight, well, belly roll. The third photo we deliberately left improperly rotated, so you kind of get a kink in your neck when you look at it. In short, the pictures were bad.

The profile, however, was sweet—perhaps even slightly pathetic. Samantha is kind-hearted. A widow. A rich widow. A gullible rich widow. Her profile almost reads like an invitation to take advantage of her gullibility. And her bank account.

Remember, these test profiles are extremes. It's part of the test.

Here Is Samantha's Test Profile:

I am recently widowed, lonely, ready to share life with a kind-hearted gentleman.

I don't need someone to support me. I am financially secure. My late husband made sure that I was well taken care of for the rest of my life.

I am your Martha-Stewart, Betty-Crocker type—I take great care of my home and those I love. I believe a woman's job is to take care of her man and her household. My name is Samantha. If you have taken the time to read my profile and are genuinely interested, please call me by my name.

Now that I'm alone, there are many choices to be made. Would be great to have someone trustworthy to help with all the big decisions that my husband always made. Please be a sincere gentleman who is looking for a forever relationship. No games. No scammers, no con-artists ... I want someone real who is ready for the rest of their life, a secure future of travel and togetherness, and all the comforts life has to offer two people in love.

My Interests: Travel, Wine-tasting, Exotic cars, Football, Cooking, Decorating, You

Our First Date: Dinner at a great restaurant with a view, great wine, great conversation, and I pick up the tab.

The 80/20 Rule In Action

Samantha's profile was pretty great. But she received less than ten percent of the messages Doreen did. It seems the pictures prevented a lot of guys from taking the time to read her profile and realize she would be a pretty great catch! As expected, the terrible photos failed to attract many messages.

Not As Clueless

Perhaps the good news is that the gentlemen who made it through the filter of bad photos were a bit more attentive to the profile. Compared to the less than nine percent who responded with Doreen's name, a "mere" 60 percent of respondents failed the name-test inside the written profile, while 40 percent of respondents used Samantha's name in their message to her, which was specifically requested in the brief profile.

The Sad Truth

Our test profiles did, indeed, prove that great photos are quite important. The sad truth is that another glaring fact showed up in every test we did: Most guys apparently didn't spend too much time reading the profiles!

One man who contacted Samantha seven times, still never used her name. His profile had no photos; he claimed he did not know how to add pictures to his profile or attach pics to his messages. A few days later, his profile mysteriously disappeared.

Here Are Some Messages "Samantha" Received:

- "Hi Samantha I'm serious I'm looking for love someone who accepts me for me I would like to get to know you more but I need to be honest with u I was shot in Afghanistan and lost control of my bladder so I have to wear diapers but no one wants to give me a chance I think your very beautiful I love your smile

- "Samantha, I'm Francis. After looking at your profile, I just wanted to say how pretty you are. I would like to get to know you. You have an interesting attitude and a really great outlook on life. Let's spend some time together. I hope to hear back from you."

Experiment #2: Professional Photos Vs. Selfies

To further test the importance of photographs, Test Profiles #3 and #4 were a warm, friendly, likable profile of a pretty girl, "Lana." The same profile, with different photos of Lana, was posted in two similar communities in neighboring states. One profile included three professional photographs, showing Lana at her best. Nothing suggestive, just pretty. The second profile included just one photo: a "selfie" of Lana wearing sunglasses.

Men in each community wrote similar messages in

response to Lana's profiles. In a 48-hour period, the profile with professional photos received two and a half times as many messages as the "selfie" profile. However, they both received a surprising amount of polite, well-written messages.

Clearly, the profile with professional photos yielded more results, allowing "Lana" the opportunity to be much more selective about her potential suitors, based on numbers, alone. Here's the proof that better photos yield better results when all other factors are the same.

Common Fixes for Common Problems

Boot The Booty Calls

Choose your words carefully. They may be sending a different message than you intended. "Hey, sexy" tends to steer things more toward a booty call, or getting blocked.

An Imaginary Barrier

If you have trouble with too many folks contacting you wanting just a friends-with-benefits (FWB) type of relationship, consider an imaginary barrier. In your profile, create a reason why you won't be able to go out with anyone for a few weeks or perhaps even a few months (for example: out of town, on vacation, big project at work, etc.) Potential suitors who only desire a physical relationship usually want these types of relations tonight or tomorrow night or perhaps this weekend and would be unwilling to wait a few weeks, let alone a month or so. They most likely will move on to easier, more immediately available prey. If you decide to go this route, you should include another hidden message in your profile to be sure they've read your profile and are aware that you are currently unavailable for dating.

Catfish Tales

Unfortunately, an environment that allows anonymity opens the door for deception. It's sad but true that some folks lie in their profiles. Some even go as far as pretending to be someone else, perhaps even someone of a different gender than they really are. They fabricate profiles (one person may have many) to hide their identity in the hope of gaining your trust and scamming you in some way. This method is called "catfishing" or being "catfished." No matter how dire the circumstances appear, you should never ever send money or gifts to someone you have never actually met. These perpetrators may do this for a living and have been honing their skills in the art of deception for years. They can be very convincing about why they are the exception to the rule, amidst a once-in-a-lifetime dilemma, and that you should bend this rule for them.

Check In

When you decide to first meet someone in person, choose a public location. Let a friend know where you are going and who you will be with, name, phone number, etc. Also, let your date know that you are doing this for safety. If your date has trouble being understanding about this, Red Flag! Check in with your friend afterward to let them know you have arrived back home safely.

It's ok to have your friend call you during the date to check on you. Keep this conversation short, just let them know that things are going as expected. This actually gives you the opportunity to let your date see you smile while telling your friend how much fun you are having!

And just in case things aren't going well, this could be an easy out. You can use the phone call/text as a trigger to end the date early. Politely excuse yourself. If you're cutting the date

Common Fixes for Common Problems

short, you might want to pay your portion of the check before you exit to avoid any hard feelings.

Keep in mind, brevity is very important. Refer to Protocol #67: Engage With Your Date, Not Your Phone.

Finally #101 …

PROTOCOL #101:
Getting a Good Partner and Keeping a Good Partner are Horses of Different Colors

Once you've found a good partner online, then what? Well, there might be other books for that! Today, online dating has spawned many happy marriages. So use the tips in this book to help you meet that special someone. When you meet a good potential forever partner, then all the rules for relationships apply. Even if your inbox is filled with potential suitors, avoid being a bright-shiny-object sort of person. You're better than that! Relationships shouldn't be disposable. Focus on the person that's right in front of you! The grass is not always greener … Remember Protocol #35: Jesus Doesn't Online Date. Nobody's perfect, including you! So don't be in too big of a hurry to move on to the next one. This book is to help you find a good partner, because if you don't find a good partner, you're certainly never going to keep one.

Glossary

Glossary

Terms and abbreviations you should know when starting to online date:

420 friendly: ok with someone who uses marijuana

ASAP: as soon as possible

ASL: age, sex (gender), location

BBW: big beautiful woman

BF: boyfriend

BHM: big handsome man

BI: bi-sexual

Booty call: request for casual sex

Catfish: internet predator who fabricates online identities

DAF: divorced Asian female

DAM: divorced Asian male

DBF: divorced black female

DBM: divorced black male

DDF: drug and disease free

DHF: divorced Hispanic female

DHM: divorced Hispanic male

DL: down low (keeping it a secret)

DTE: down-to-earth

Dutch: each person pays their own way

DWF: divorced white female

DWM: divorced white male

F2F: face to face (meeting in person)

FB: Facebook

FWB: friends with benefits, commonly used when a casual sexual partner is being sought

FYI: for your information

GF: girlfriend

HET: heterosexual

HWP: height/weight proportional

IDK: I don't know

IMO: in my opinion

ISO: in search of

LDR: long-distance relationship

LMAO: laughing my butt off

LTR: long-term relationship

Match: Match.com, dating website

M4M: man seeking men

NS: nonsmoking

NSA: no strings attached

PDA: public display of affection

POF: PlentyofFish.com, dating website

SAF: single Asian female

SAM: single Asian male

SBF: Single black female

SBM: Single black male

Selfie: a photo you have taken of yourself

SHF: single Hispanic female

SHM: single Hispanic male

S&M: sadomasochism

STD: sexually transmitted disease

STR8: straight

Sugar daddy: male willing to financially support someone

SWF: single white female

SWM: single white male

SWS: sex without strings (casual sex)

TLC: tender loving care

TMI: too much information

TTYL: talk to you later

TX: thank you

W4W: woman seeking women

WLTM: would like to meet

WTF: what the f**k

XOXO: hugs and kisses

About the Author

Brent Louis Miller was a pioneer in his early college years, founding a precursor to online dating, Dial-A-Date. Years later, he owned a franchise of a speed-dating service, where people meet potential suitors face to face in quick, three-minute bursts.

Brent is a bookstore owner, photographer, actor, pilot, singer/songwriter, stand-up comedian, and golfer, who loves to travel. He lives in Nashville, Tennessee, "Music City," and is working on his next book.

Made in the USA
Middletown, DE
27 November 2017